OF MICE AND MEN

AN ESSAY WRITING GUIDE FOR GCSE

R. P. DAVIS

Published by Accolade Tuition Ltd
71-75 Shelton Street
Covent Garden
London WC2H 9JQ
www.accoladetuition.com
info@accoladetuition.com

ISBN 978-1-913988-18-0

FIRST EDITION
1 3 5 7 9 10 8 6 4 2

CONTENTS

FOREWORD FOR EDEXCEL IGCSE STUDENTS

In your IGCSE English Literature exam, you will be presented with two questions on John Steinbeck's *Of Mice and Men*, and you will then be asked to pick just one to answer. Of course, once you've picked the question you prefer, there are many methods you might use to tackle it. However, there is one particular technique which, due to its sophistication, most readily allows students to unlock the highest marks: namely, the thematic method.

To be clear, this study guide is not intended to walk you through the play act-by-act and sequence-by-sequence: there are many great guides out there that do just that. No, this guide, by sifting through a series of mock exam questions, will demonstrate how to organise a response thematically and thus write a stellar essay: a skill we believe no other study guide adequately covers!

I have encountered students who have structured their essays all sorts of ways: some who'll write about the play chronologically, others who'll give each character their own paragraph. The method I'm advocating, on the other hand, involves picking out three to four themes that will allow you to holistically answer the question: these three to four themes will become the three to four content paragraphs of your essay, cushioned between a brief introduction and conclusion. Ideally, these themes will follow from one to the next to create a flowing argument. Within each of these thematic paragraphs, you can then ensure you are jumping through the mark scheme's hoops.

The Steinbeckian equivalent of a selfie.

So to break things down further, each thematic paragraph will include various point-scoring components. In each paragraph, you will include quotes from the novel (yes, that means you'll have to have some committed to memory!), offer analyses of these quotes, and discuss how they illustrate the theme you're discussing. And in every paragraph, you will comment on the era in which the novel was written and how that helps to understand the chosen theme.

Don't worry if this all feels daunting. Throughout this guide, I will be illustrating in great detail – by means of examples – how to build an essay of this kind.

The beauty of the thematic approach is that, once you have your themes, you suddenly have a direction and a trajectory, and this makes essay writing a whole lot easier. However, it must also be noted that selecting themes in the first place is something students often find tricky. I have come across many candidates who understand the play inside out; but when they are presented with questions under exam conditions, and the pressure kicks in, they find it tough to break their response down into themes. The fact of the matter is: the process is a creative one and the best themes require a bit of imagination.

In this guide, I shall take different exam-style questions, and shall put together a plan for each – a plan that illustrates in detail how we will be satisfying the mark scheme's criteria. Please do keep in mind that, when operating under timed conditions, your plans will necessarily be less detailed than those that appear in this volume.

A mural outside the Steinbeck museum in Salinas, California. To the bottom left, you can see Lenny and George walking side by side. In the centre, of course, is Steinbeck himself. Copyright © Joe Flood

Now, you might be asking whether three or four themes is best. The truth is, you should do whatever you feel most comfortable with: the examiner is looking for an original, creative answer, and not sitting there counting the themes. So if you think you are quick enough to cover four, then great. However, if you would rather do three to make sure you do each theme justice, that's also fine. I sometimes suggest that my students pick four themes, but make the fourth one smaller – sort of like an afterthought, or an observation that turns things on their head. That way, if they feel they won't have time to explore this fourth theme in its own right, they can always give it a quick mention in the conclusion instead.

Before I move forward in earnest, I believe it to be worthwhile to run through the two Assessment Objectives the exam board want you to cover in your response – if only to demonstrate how effective the thematic response can be. I would argue that the first Assessment Objective (AO1) – the one that wants candidates to 'demonstrate a close knowledge and understanding of the text' while 'maintaining a critical style' and which is worth 20 of the total 40 marks up for grabs – will be wholly satisfied by selecting strong themes, then fleshing them out with quotes. For one thing, themes are perhaps the best way to demonstrate an 'understanding of the text', since themes are the foundation on which any text is built. For another, Edexcel mark schemes have sections entitled 'indicative content' to help examiners award AO1 marks, and this contains a list of (you've guessed it) themes and concepts students might have picked out.

Indeed, one chief examiner has explicitly noted that to 'explore a number of themes' will nudge a candidate towards the top grade band.

The second Assessment Objective you will be graded on is AO4, which requires students to 'show understanding of the relationships between texts and the contexts in which they were written' – and this one is responsible for another 20 of the 40 marks. Context observations – as I'll demonstrate – are so much easier to weave into a theme-based essay; indeed, the theme gives the student a chance to bring up context in a relevant and fitting way. After all, you don't want it to look like you've just shoehorned a contextual factoid into the mix.

John Steinbeck's grave in Salinas, California. Copyright © Naotake Murayama

---

My hope is that this book, by demonstrating how to select relevant themes, will help you feel more confident in doing so yourself. I believe it is also worth mentioning that the themes I have picked out are by no means definitive. Asked the very same question, someone else may pick out different themes, and write an answer that is just as good (if not better!). Obviously the exam is not likely to be fun – my memory of them is pretty much the exact opposite. But still, this is one of the very few chances that you will get at GCSE level to actually be creative.

And to my mind at least, that was always more enjoyable – if enjoyable is the right word – than simply demonstrating that I had memorised loads of facts.

NB: There is a brief second section at the end of this guide. You can disregard this section, however, since it is only applicable to students working towards the WJEC GCSE!

FOREWORD FOR WJEC STUDENTS

In your GCSE English Literature exam, you will be required to tackle two questions on John Steinbeck's *Of Mice and Men*: one shorter question (worth 10 marks) that revolves around an extract from the novel, and one longer question (worth 20 marks) that relates to the novel as a whole. There are of course many methods you might use to tackle these questions. However, there is one particular technique which, due to its sophistication, most readily allows students to unlock the highest marks: namely, the thematic method.

This guide is split into two parts. First, we will be dealing with the 20 mark questions. Because this is worth the lion's share of the marks, this section of the guide is the chunkiest. Next, there is a shorter section dedicated to the 10 mark extract-based question.

To be clear, this study guide is not intended to walk you through the novel chapter-by-chapter and sequence-by-sequence: there are many great guides out there that do just that. No, this guide, by sifting through a series of mock exam questions, will demonstrate how to organise a response thematically and thus write a stellar essay: a skill we believe no other study guide adequately covers!

The 20 mark (whole novel) question

Let's pause for a moment on the 20 mark question.

In the exam, you will in fact be given a choice of *two* 20 mark questions, and you will be invited to pick the one you prefer.

A bust of Steinbeck in Monterey, California. Copyright © Marco

Now, I have encountered students who have structured these longer essays all sorts of ways: some who'll write about the novel chronologically, others who'll give each character their own paragraph. The method I'm advocating, on the other hand, involves picking out three to four themes that will allow you to holistically answer the question: these three to four themes will become the three to four content paragraphs of your essay, cushioned between a brief introduction and conclusion. Ideally, these themes will follow from one to the next to create a flowing argument. Within each of these thematic paragraphs, you can then ensure you are jumping through the mark scheme's hoops.

So to break things down further, each thematic paragraph will include various point-scoring components. In each paragraph, you will include quotes from the novel (yes, that means you'll have to have some committed to memory!), offer analyses of these quotes, and discuss how they illustrate the theme you're discussing. And in every paragraph, you will comment on the era in which the novel was written and how that helps to understand the chosen theme.

Don't worry if this all feels daunting. Throughout this guide, I will be illustrating in great detail – by means of examples – how to build an essay of this kind.

The beauty of the thematic approach is that, once you have your themes, you suddenly have a direction and a trajectory, and this makes essay writing a whole lot easier. However, it must also be noted that selecting themes in the first place is something students often find tricky. I have come across many candidates who understand the novel inside out; but when they are presented with questions under exam conditions, and the pressure kicks in, they find it tough to break their response down into themes. The fact of the matter is: the process is a creative one and the best themes require a bit of imagination.

In this guide, I shall take different exam-style questions, and shall put together a plan for each – a plan that illustrates in detail how we will be satisfying the mark scheme's criteria. Please do keep in mind that, when operating under timed conditions, your plans will necessarily be less detailed than those that appear in this volume.

Steinbeck's boyhood home in Salinas, California. Copyright © Naotake Murayama

Now, you might be asking whether three or four themes is best. The truth is, you should do whatever you feel most comfortable with: the examiner is looking for an original, creative answer, and not sitting there counting the themes. So if you think you are quick enough to cover four, then great. However, if you would rather do three to make sure you do each theme justice, that's also fine. I sometimes suggest that my student pick four themes, but make the fourth one smaller – sort of like an afterthought, or an observation that turns things on their head. That way, if they feel they won't have time to explore this fourth theme in its own right, they can always give it a quick mention in the conclusion instead.

It is instructive at this point, I believe, to run through the Assessment Objectives in the mark scheme – if only to demonstrate how effective the thematic response can be. I would argue that the first Assessment Objective (AO1) – the one that wants candidates to 'respond to texts critically and imaginatively' and which is worth a third of the marks in the 20-mark question – will be wholly satisfied by selecting strong themes, then fleshing them out with quotes. Indeed, when it comes to identifying the top scoring candidates for AO1, the mark scheme explicitly tells examiners to look for a response that 'convey[s] ideas persuasively and cogently with apt textual support' – the word 'idea' is a synonym of theme, and 'apt textual support' simply refers to quotes that appropriately support the theme you've chosen.

The other Assessment Objective that you need to be aware of for the 20 mark question is AO4, which requires students to 'relate texts to their social, cultural and historical contexts' and 'explain how texts have been influential and significant to... readers in different contexts and at different times' – this is responsible for the other two-thirds of the marks in play. The good news is that comments on context are easy enough to weave into a thematic argument; indeed, the theme gives the student a chance to bring up context in a relevant and fitting way. After all, you don't want it to look like you've just shoehorned a contextual factoid into the mix.

The 10 mark (extract-based) question

In the second part of this guide, we will look at extract-based (10 mark) questions.

Again, we will be structuring our responses using the thematic method; after all, 5 of the 10 marks at play in this question are awarded for AO1; and, as explained already, the thematic method is our best way of hitting the exam board's AO1 criteria. However, because these extract-based questions are worth fewer marks all in all, we will be dealing with each theme in a shorter and sharper fashion.

A key thing to keep in mind with the 10 mark question, though, is that you *do not* need to invoke historical context (or AO4). Instead, the other 5 marks in play are for AO2, which asks candidates to 'explain how language, structure and form contribute to writers' presentation of ideas [and] themes.'

A plaque in Manhattan, New York, at the location where Steinbeck lived for a period. Copyright © Brian Cooper

Now, you will already be quoting from the extract as you back up your themes, and it is a fairly natural progression to then analyse the language techniques used. Indeed, allowing a thematic discussion to lead your close language analysis is far more effective than simply observing language techniques (metaphor here, alliteration there), because by discussing how the language techniques relate to and shape the theme, you will be more directly meeting the exam board's criteria: namely, to look at how language 'contribute[s] to [the] presentation of ideas [and] themes'.

In my experience, language analysis is the most important element of AO4 – perhaps 3 of the 5 marks will go towards language analysis. You will also notice, however, that AO4 asks students to comment on 'structure and form.' Again, the thematic approach has your back – because though simply jamming in a point on structure or form will feel jarring, when you bring these points up while discussing a theme, as a means to further a thematic argument, you will again organically be discussing the way it 'contributes to [the] presentation of ideas [and] themes].'

Final comment

My hope is that this book, by demonstrating how to select relevant themes, will help you feel more confident in doing so yourself. I believe it is also worth mentioning that the themes I have picked out are by no means definitive. Asked the very same question, someone else may pick out different themes, and write an answer that is just as good (if not better!). Obviously the exam is not likely to be fun – my memory of them is pretty much the exact opposite. But still, this is one of the very few chances that you will get at GCSE level to actually be creative. And to my mind at least, that was always more enjoyable – if enjoyable is the right word – than simply demonstrating that I had memorised loads of facts.

PART ONE

ESSAY PLAN ONE

HOW DOES JOHN STEINBECK INSPIRE SYMPATHY FOR LENNIE IN OF MICE AND MEN?

Introduction

A great way to approach your introduction is to use context as a springboard – that way, you are meeting the exam board's AO4 criteria right off the bat. On this occasion, I've decided to meditate on the economic circumstances in which the novel was written, while briefly nodding to literary context, too. I then pivot into a quick summary of the themes I intend to cover.

> 'Given the brutal economic conditions that befell America in the decade following 1929's Wall Street Crash – a decade characterised by mass unemployment, food-shortages and pervasive homelessness – it is perhaps unsurprising that there came an outpouring of literature (such as Robert Cantwell's *The Land of Plenty* and Steinbeck's *Of Mice and Men*) that sympathetically explored the lives of those weathering such circumstances. Yet while Lennie's status as lowly itinerant worker in *Of Mice*

and Men immediately serves to invite sympathy, Steinbeck – by characterising Lennie as a kind of overwhelmed divine fool, and intimately charting George's sympathies for his companion – strives to inspire a more complicated, heightened sympathy for Lennie.[1]

Theme/Paragraph One: By prioritising George's perception of Lennie – and exploring in-depth both George's sympathy for and exasperation with Lennie – Steinbeck invites the reader to vicariously experience these feelings, too.[2]

- Though the text is written in the third person, the reader's perception of Lennie is mediated throughout via George.[3] The first words George speaks are an assessment of Lennie's behaviour and conduct: he 'sharply' reprimands Lennie for drinking the water to excess: 'You gonna be sick like you was last night.' George's exasperation, then, functions as a prompt for readers. Moments later, however, George's exasperation is complicated by a distinct strain of sympathy: as Lennie (naively believing George to be oblivious) goes to retrieve the mouse George hurled away, Lennie soliloquises his true sense of sympathy for Lennie: '"Poor bastard," he said softly'.[4] [*AO1 for elaborating on my theme and invoking relevant quotations to buttress my argument*].
- George's sympathy for Lennie is a prompt that persists throughout the novel. Even at the point in the novel at which our sympathy for Lennie is most

strained – in the wake of his killing Curley's wife – George still sympathises with Lennie: he worries that 'the poor barstad'd starve' if left on his own, and insists 'Lennie never done it in meanness'. [*Further AO1 for adding complexity to the argument and, again, deploying textual evidence*].

- By using Lennie's closest friend as a means to inspire sympathy, Steinbeck arguably rebukes the philosophy of rugged individualism that pervaded American culture throughout the early twentieth century: a philosophy that tacitly eschewed sympathy for one's fellow man, instead preaching a gospel of prioritising oneself above all others.[5] That Herbert Hoover (the originator of the term rugged individualism) was defeated in the 1932 presidential election by Franklin Roosevelt – a big-government Democrat, whose politics sought to help the needy – indicates that Steinbeck, with his rebuke, was part of a wider popular movement seeking to challenge the dogma of individualism.[6] [*AO4 for coherently enhancing my argument with relevant historical context*].

Theme/Paragraph Two: We are given direct insight into Lennie's mental state and processes: we can see the naivety and simplicity that makes him a sympathetic being.

- While the reader's perception of Lennie is mediated through George, Steinbeck on a number of occasions gives the reader a direct insight into Lennie's mental state: and Lennie's childlike naivety in the face of a cruel, uncaring world fosters sympathy, forcing the reader to empathise with his unique plight. [*AO1 for deploying a theme that showcases my understanding of the novel*].

- The reader's most persistent window into Lennie's mindset is his words – particularly his refrain about the 'rabbits' he hopes to someday tend to: he expresses his 'wish' to get 'the rabbits pretty soon' in the opening chapter; in Chapter Three, he wonders 'how long's it gonna be till' he has his 'rabbits'; and in Chapter Four he boisterously tells Crooks 'Bout the rabbits'. In the wake of the 1862 Homestead Act, a homestead ethic developed on the American frontier, which construed the right to own a farm and be financially autonomous and safe from violence as sacrosanct.[7] Lennie's talk of the rabbits is his childlike way of expressing his yearning for precisely this right; and, given the mythic power of the homestead ethic, a contemporary audience would have been particularly sympathetic to the impossibility of his longings. [*AO4 for coherently enhancing my argument with relevant historical context*].
- At the start of the final chapter, Lennie holds court with first a projection of his 'Aunt Clara', and next a 'gigantic rabbit'. That his mind conjures a giant rabbit in the first place infantilises Lennie, heightening our sympathy for this naïve, childlike individual. That this gigantic rabbit, the arch symbol of Lennie's homestead longings, proceeds to rebuke and taunt him – 'he [George] is gonna leave ya' – provokes further sympathy: the mythic homestead is closed off from Lennie forever. [*AO1 for elaborating on my theme and invoking relevant quotations to buttress my argument; AO4 for enhancing my argument with relevant historical context*].

Theme/Paragraph Three: Steinbeck also provokes sympathy for Lennie by placing him at the receiving end of physical violence.

- Near the close of Chapter Three, Curley, in an act of unprovoked violence, explosively sets upon Lennie, and the focus is placed squarely on the profundity of Lennie's fear: Lennie's terror is reiterated multiple times – 'Lennie gave a cry of terror'; 'Lennie...bleated with terror' – and we are told explicitly that 'he was too frightened to defend himself'. Curiously, even when Lennie eventually defends himself (he crushes Curley's hand with excessive force), Steinbeck continues to keep the focus on Lennie's terror: 'Lennie watched in terror the flopping little man'. Cumulatively, the effect is to induce sympathy for Lennie: he is the victim of violence he can barely understand, and incapable of responding to proportionately. [*AO1 for elaborating on my theme and invoking relevant quotations to buttress my argument*].
- It ought to be noted that in the early twentieth century there persisted what historians call the 'code of the West', which conceived of male-on-male violence as only permissible when deployed in self-defence and required fair play. That Curley's attack so plainly transgresses this 'code' further arouses sympathy for Lennie.[8] [*AO4 for coherently enhancing my argument with relevant historical context*].
- Of course, there are times when Lennie in fact initiates violence: most notably, in the sequence that sees him snap Curley's wife's neck. Yet while this incident in some respects strains our sympathies for

Lennie – and, at the very least, Curley's wife becomes the focal point of our sympathies – Steinbeck nevertheless strives to define Lennie's violence in opposition to Curley's (it is borne of panic as opposed to malice) and to emphasise Lennie's lack of agency. [*AO1 for cogently elaborating on my theme*].

Theme/Paragraph Four: We are invited to feel sympathy for Lennie due to symbolic associations. He is linked to Candy's dog through their shared means of death; he is linked also to Candy, Crooks and Curley's wife – other pitiable, ostracised individuals.

- In Chapter Three, Candy's dog – who had previously been described as 'ancient' and with 'mild, half-blind eyes' – is taken outside and shot "off-stage" in an instance of shocking violence. However, the sympathy we feel for this defenceless dog does not exist in a vacuum; rather, when, in the novel's final chapter, Lennie is killed in near-identical fashion – a bullet 'where the spin and skull were joined' – the reader is forced to place Lennie in the same symbolic bracket as Candy's dog: both pitiable living creatures for whom the world is too cruel. [*AO1 for elaborating on my theme and invoking relevant quotations to buttress my argument*].
- If Lennie is symbolically entangled with Candy's dog, he is entangled, too, with the human outcasts of the novel. In Chapter Four, when the lion's share of the ranch-hands have temporarily decamped to Soledad, the "misfits" – Lennie, Candy and Crooks – assemble

in Crooks's bedroom: as Curley's wife put it, 'they left all the weak ones here' (and since we know Lennie is in fact colossally strong, we can infer that she is referring to Lennie's more intangible weaknesses). Insofar as Candy, a crippled old man, and Crooks, the lone representative of a black America in the land of punitive Jim Crow, warrant our sympathy, Lennie's symbolic association with them here functions to arouse our sympathy for him as well.[9] Indeed, though Curley's wife sees herself as apart from these three men, she too is an ostracised, pitiable figure as the lone woman on a ranch that is in many ways a microcosm of a brutally patriarchal society – and, again, her presence deepens our sympathy for the entire foursome.[10] [*AO1 for elaborating on my theme and invoking relevant quotations to buttress my argument; AO4 for enhancing my argument with relevant historical context*].

Conclusion

When possible, it's great to give the examiner something new in the conclusion (as opposed to simply repeating what you have said already). On this occasion, I start by making the argument that Lennie in a sense is a bit like a reader: he is on the receiving end of stories of the American dream. Then, to ensure that nobody can accuse me of not adequately focusing on context and AO4, I invoke contemporary cultural concerns as well as a piece of literary context.

'Time and again throughout the novel, Lennie functions as a kind of surrogate reader, on the receiving end of a story spun by George of a 'little house and a couple of acres'. In a sense, then, we feel sorry for Lennie insofar as he is the American everyman, a forerunner of Miller's Willy Loman, who has been sold the illusory story of the American dream – a story that became all the more preposterous during the Great Depression.[11] Steinbeck's novel, it seems, is inviting us to sympathise not just with Lennie-the-surrogate-reader, but also with his contemporary readership *en masse*: the huddled masses for whom the story of the American dream proved painfully hollow.'

A 1939 image of a shantytown in Seattle, Washington – known also (in a damning indictment of the then ex-President's policies) as a Hooverville. In the wake of the Wall Street Crash, many wound up homeless, and Hoovervilles sprung up around the country. Copyright © Seattle Municipal Archives

ESSAY PLAN TWO

'DREAMS ALWAYS RESULT IN TRAGEDY IN OF MICE AND MEN.' TO WHAT EXTENT DO YOU AGREE WITH THIS STATEMENT?

Introduction

When it comes to historical context, you do not need to reinvent the wheel. The Great Depression is something I constantly allude to throughout this guide – yes, it's obvious, but it's also essential to understanding this novel, so don't shy away from bringing it up!

'While the concept of the American Dream – the notion that anyone willing to work could achieve economically – was at the centre of American consciousness throughout the twentieth century, the Great Depression of the 1930s profoundly undercut its premise, as the country grappled with diminishing economic opportunities. In *Of Mice and Men*, those characters who harbour dreams and ambitions of economic betterment do indeed meet tragic ends; however, it could be argued that these characters have been trapped in tragic circumstances in the first place, and that their dreams and ambitions are not so much catalysts of tragedy, but tools that help them cope with tragic circumstances.'

Theme/Paragraph One: Those who harbour aspirations meet tragic ends: Lennie, George, Candy, Curley's wife. Although there is not often a direct cause and effect, the fullness of this pattern seems to implicitly suggest a link.

- The aspiration that lies at the heart of the novel is George and Lennie's desire to purchase a 'little house and a couple of acres' and 'live on the fatta the land'. It is, in many respects, the epitome of the American dream on the frontier, where personal property (particularly in the wake of the 1862 Homestead Act) signified sovereignty and autonomy. Later, Candy is permitted to share in this dream, after committing the 'two hundred an' fifty dollars' compensation for losing his hand. Yet all three characters meet tragic ends. The execution of Lennie in the final chapter is tragic for both Lennie and George – the former loses his life; the latter is forced by circumstance to slay his life-long companion – and the fact George is outlining their ambitions to distract Lennie as this takes place tacitly suggests a through-line between their aspirations and this tragic denouement.[1] [*AO1 for elaborating on my theme and invoking relevant quotations to buttress my argument; AO4 for enhancing my argument with relevant historical context*].
- While not so emphatic, Candy's fate is also tragic: we

are left to assume, as Crooks put it, that he will be forced to 'be a swamper...till they take [him] out in a box'. [*Further AO1 for adding complexity to the argument and, again, deploying textual evidence*].

- Although Curley's wife harbours her own, separate set of ambitions (as she tells Lennie, she longs to have 'been in movies' and own 'nice clothes'), it is significant that Steinbeck ensures that she, too, meets a tragic end: she winds up dead under 'a half-covering of yellow hay'. The forcefulness of the pattern arguably suggests that, although the cause and effect between these ambitions and tragic outcomes is not always clear, Steinbeck wishes us to perceive a link between the two. [*Further AO1 for adding complexity to the argument and, again, deploying textual evidence*].

Theme/Paragraph Two: Arguably aspirations are not so much what causes tragedy, but a buffer to help all the individuals cope with their already tragic circumstances: that is to say, we find the characters from the outset in a state of tragedy.

- In the wake of the Dust Bowl droughts in the Midwest and South (which took place throughout the 1930s), a number of desperate, out-of-work migrants (known as Okies) headed to California, and their circumstances there from the outset were extremely tragic: their livelihoods had been wrecked and they were consigned to brutal labour. [*AO4 for invoking historical context that is relevant to the discussion at hand*].

- Steinbeck dealt with the plight of the Okies explicitly in *The Grapes of Wrath*. However, many of the poor labourers in *Of Mice and Men*, while perhaps not identified as Okies, face a similarly tragic set of circumstances from the very beginning. In consequence, it could be argued that Steinbeck does not wish for us to see their aspirations as responsible for tragedy; rather, by having so many of his characters trapped in tragic circumstances in the first place, Steinbeck arguably presents dreams as coping mechanisms that helps individuals survive their circumstances. In the opening chapter, we find Lennie and George in dire straits analogous to those of the Okies: short on cash, sleeping rough, and longing for the small luxury of ketchup. Yet as George narrates the outlines of their grand dream, there is a sense of escapism: George 'repeated his words rhythmically', as those hypnotising his present woes away, and Lennie is 'delighted'. [*AO1 for elaborating on my theme and invoking relevant quotations to buttress my argument; AO4 for enhancing my argument with relevant historical and literary context*].
- This pattern of deploying these daydreams as a coping mechanism recurs time and again: in Chapter Three, shortly after Candy's dog is executed, Candy, George and Lennie all find themselves 'bemused by the beauty' of aspirations, thereby granting them temporary relief. Candy is unable to help bringing up the 'rabbits' – shorthand for their aspirations – in front of Crooks in Chapter Four; and, arguably, George rehashes their ambitions in the final chapter as a means of giving Lennie one last dose of happiness before his demise. [*Further AO1 for adding*

complexity to the argument and, again, deploying textual evidence].

Theme/Paragraph Three: Perhaps more tragic than unfulfilled aspirations is the circumstance of not being permitted to have aspirations in the first place – which is the case for Crooks.

- In Chapter Four, after Candy and Lennie briefly detail their aspirations, Crooks momentarily finds himself buying into the fantasy, and he diffidently puts himself forward: 'If you... guys would want a hand to work for nothing', he offers. Yet mere moments later, as if a punishment for daring to dream, Crooks finds himself on the receiving end of Curley's wife's vitriolic racial abuse: she threatens to have him lynched – 'I could get you strung up on a tree' – and Steinbeck describes Curley's wife as at the ready to 'whip at him again', as if her words were emulating the whips used to torture slaves in antebellum America.[2] [*AO1 for elaborating on my theme and invoking relevant quotations to buttress my argument; AO4 for enhancing my argument with relevant historical context*].
- After Crooks has 'reduced himself to nothing' in the wake of this abuse, he recants his aspirations: 'I didn' mean it'. It is not that dreams are responsible for begetting tragedy, this sequence seems to suggest; rather, the true tragedy is not being permitted to entertain aspirations in the first place. [*Further AO1 for adding complexity to the argument and, again, deploying textual evidence*].
- Certainly, the violence and lack of opportunities

Crooks faces tallies with the realities of 1930s America: black Americans faced extreme economic hardship (by 1932, half of all black Americans were out of work) and mounting violence (lynching increasing more than fourfold between 1932 and 1933). In short, America was a place where black Americans truly did not have room for aspirations; as James Baldwin, a seminal writer who came of age in the 1930s would later note, any given black American had been born into a 'society which spelled out with brutal clarity... that [they] were a worthless human being [and]...not expected to aspire'. [*AO4 for enhancing my argument with relevant historical and literary context*].

Conclusion

Remember, context comes in many different shapes and forms. You can score AO4 marks not only by referring to events that were unfolding at the time, but also by discussing cultural attitudes as well as the work of other authors/artists of the period. Here, for instance, I bring in another text that was written in the same year and which deals with some very similar themes.

'In Clifford Odets's play *Golden Boy* – which, like *Of Mice and Men*, was published in 1937, and was intended as a cautionary tale about the chimera of the American Dream – the fiercely aspirational boxer, Joe Bonaparte, meets a tragic fate in a car crash, the pattern suggesting that aspiration and tragedy go hand in hand.[3] Whether we interpret aspirations in Steinbeck's novel as similarly a catalyst for tragedy, or as a means of psychologically escaping tragic circumstances – or perhaps, paradoxically, both – it is undoubtedly the case that the tragic circumstances in which we find most of the *dramatis personae* at the novel's start deteriorate still further as the narrative unfolds.'

The Dust Bowl draughts led to devastating conditions, as seen in the photo above.

ESSAY PLAN THREE

HOW DOES JOHN STEINBECK USE THE CHARACTER OF CURLEY'S WIFE TO HIGHLIGHT SOME ASPECTS OF AMERICAN SOCIETY IN THE 1930S?

Introduction

AO4 accounts for many of the marks in this essay, so don't shy away from grabbing those context marks straight out of the gate. You can see that on this occasion I intermingle discussions of contemporary attitudes with solid historical facts, then use this as a means to segue into the themes my essay will cover. Hopefully you can see that there is a formula that underpins what I'm doing.

'Whereas the "Roaring Twenties" saw women challenge certain gender expectations – the iconic Flapper, for instance, became a symbol of liberated female sexuality – the 1930s marked a reactionary backlash, with the inception of such institutions as The National Institute of Decency, an organisation dedicated to cleansing film of any gender representation they deemed risqué. Curley's wife – with her exclusion from male-centred spaces, her financial dependency on her husband, and the sense of scandal her sexuality elicits – illustrates many of the challenges women faced in 1930s.'

Theme/Paragraph One: Curley's wife is excluded from male-dominated places of work, and expected to confine herself to the domestic sphere – a reflection of how women were ostracised from contemporary workforces and forced into economic dependence.

- From Curley's wife's very first appearance, Steinbeck telegraphs her exclusion from the male sphere: she does not enter the men's bunk room, but is instead seen at the threshold 'standing there looking in'. The stagecraft here relays that, though Curley's wife wishes to challenge strictures, she is still symbolically kept at bay. Steinbeck deploys the self-same symbolism again, when, in Chapter Four, she is seen 'still in the doorway'. However, what this symbolism relays subtly, George states explicitly elsewhere: 'Ranch with a bunch of guys on it ain't no place for a girl'. [*AO1 for elaborating on my theme and invoking relevant quotations to buttress my argument*].
- Tacit in this expectation that Curley's wife remain in the domestic space, and keep clear of the male-centric workspace – to 'stick in that house', as Curley's wife puts it – is that she must remain economically dependent on her husband. Indeed, this dependency is encoded into her name, which casts her as her

husband's property, and anticipates the naming conventions in Atwood's *The Handmaid's Tale.*[1] [*Further AO1 for adding complexity to the argument and, again, deploying textual evidence; AO4 for enhancing my argument with relevant literary context*].

- Curley's wife's exclusion from the workplace – and thus the means of economic autonomy – mirrors the systematic exclusion from the workplace women endured during Roosevelt's New Deal. For instance, his Civil Conservation Corps – a huge programme launched to provide work for urban-dwellers – at first completely excluded women, before eventually allowing extremely limited enrolment for women, who, unlike their male counterparts, received an allowance as opposed to a wage. [*AO4 for enhancing my argument with relevant historical context*].

Theme/Paragraph Two: The way the men scorn and rebuke Curley's wife's sexuality gives an insight into double-standards within America at the time.

- In the early 1930s, Hollywood produced a litany of films that sought to candidly explore female sexuality: 1933's *Design for Living*, for instance, centred on a woman with multiple partners, whereas *Queen Christina* (also 1933) revolved around a bisexual female protagonist. Yet these films promptly provoked a backlash, with the introduction of the Hays Code in 1934, which sought to sanitise films of any such exploration of female sexuality. [*AO4 for invoking historical and artistic context that is relevant to the discussion at hand*].

- In the same way patriarchal powers sought to police the expression of female sexuality in Hollywood, Curley's wife in *Of Mice and Men* also encounters a vicious backlash to her candid display of sexuality. After his first encounter with Curley's wife George derides her overt sexuality: he calls her a 'poison', and 'jail-bait' – words that seeks to frame female sexuality as something dangerous – and this animosity towards her as an avatar of female sexuality is echoed by others: Candy, for instance, degradingly dubs her a 'tart'.[2] Even after her tragic death, Candy keeps up this rhetoric: 'you God damn tramp'. The insinuation of his lack of sympathy is that, to his his mind, Curley's wife deserves this fate: it is the patriarchal order justly policing her sexuality. [*AO1 for elaborating on my theme and invoking relevant quotations to buttress my argument; AO4 for enhancing my argument with relevant historical and artistic context*].
- Interestingly, however, while Curley's wife is vilified and punished for her sexuality, Curley – in a way that reflected the double-standards of the 1930s – is able to commit adultery with impunity: Curley's wife is aware that 'even Curley' is visiting the brothel in Chapter Four. [*Further AO1 for adding complexity to the argument and, again, deploying textual evidence; AO4 for enhancing my argument with relevant historical context*].

Theme/Paragraph Three: Although a victim in many senses, Curley's wife's treatment of Crooks

points to the realities of racial violence in 1930s America.

- While evidence of racial animus is present from early on in the novel, the key episode that reveals the extent of this animus appears in Chapter Four: when Curley's wife verbally pillories Crooks while intruding in his bedroom.[3] Curley's wife's threat to get Crooks lynched – 'I could get you strung up on a tree' – echoes the realities in 1930s America, where accusations of wrongdoing levelled at black men by white women could indeed lead to extra-judicial violence, as evidenced by the mob who had sought to lynch a group of 11 black men and boys (known as the Scottsboro Boys) after they had been accused of rape by two white women in 1931. [*AO1 for elaborating on my theme and invoking relevant quotations to buttress my argument; AO4 for enhancing my argument with relevant historical context*].
- However, while Curley's wife's racism is front and centre in this episode, she also reveals an ageism and ableism that she has internalised from society. By the 1930s, the eugenicist Harry Loughlin had become an influential force in American life – his writings, dating back to 1914, asserted that all kinds of disabled peoples ought to be sterilised; and in fact California had sterilisation laws in place from 1909, which led to some 20,000 individuals being operated on against their will in that state alone. As a result, it is perhaps unsurprising that, just prior to her racial diatribe, Curley's wife refers to Lennie and Candy respectively as a 'dum-dum and a lousy ol' sheep'.[4] The phrase 'lousy ol' sheep' dehumanises Candy,

whereas the phrase 'dum-dum' serves to mock Lennie's limited capacity for speech.[5] Although her cruelty is undoubtedly ironic (Curley's wife is of course ostracised and disadvantaged, too) it nevertheless gestures to societal cruelties that existed in 1930s America. [*AO1 for elaborating on my theme and invoking relevant quotations to buttress my argument; AO4 for enhancing my argument with relevant historical and artistic context*].

Conclusion

I had one more argument up my sleeve – namely, that Curley's wife invites us to think about contemporary ideas regarding vigilantism – but decided that it was not meaty enough to be one of my content paragraphs. As a result, I decided to work it into my conclusion instead. That my discussion is rooted in a historical concern means that I am also picking up any AO4 marks going spare.

'In the wake of finding his wife's body, Curley is not interested in having Lennie arrested; instead, he states his intention to kill Lennie himself: 'I'll kill the big son-of-a-bitch myself'. Although Curley's is most likely acting to exact vengeance for his injured hand, Curley's wife, by giving Curley an excuse to hunt Lennie, illustrates another dimension of 1930s American life: the instinct to engage in vigilantism – which had parallels with such real-world incidents as the accosting of a group of three bank robbers in Culver, Indiana in 1933 by a vigilante posse. Indeed, Steinbeck's insights into contemporary American life go beyond the depiction of Curley's wife: the ranch as a whole at times seems as if a microcosm of 1930s American society: a utilitarian, dog-eat-dog realm where individuals are ensnared by their economic circumstance.'

A poster for the 1933 Hollywood film, *Queen Cristina* (portrayed by the actress Greta Garbo), which revolved around a bisexual protagonist. It was films like this one that triggered a scandalised backlash that led to film regulations seeking to police how female sexuality was portrayed.

ESSAY PLAN FOUR

'THE CHARACTERS IN OF MICE AND MEN ARE REPEATEDLY SHOWN TO BE POWERLESS OVER THEIR CIRCUMSTANCES.' TO WHAT EXTENT DO YOU AGREE WITH THIS STATEMENT?

Introduction

It is really useful to be aware of the politics of the time, as this is great material to deploy to pick up AO4 marks. Spend a bit of time reading up on Herbert Hoover, Franklin Roosevelt, the 1932 Presidential Election, and Roosevelt's New Deal. You don't need to be an expert, but a sound knowledge will stand you in good stead. You can see below how I use my understanding of the New Deal as a means to springboard into a discussion about Steinbeck's characters' struggle for autonomy.

'The election of Franklin Roosevelt to the White House in 1932, and the New Deal that ensued, in many respects marked an attempt to not only take back control of an atrophying economy through an unprecedented expansion of the federal government, but also to grant struggling citizens some semblance of financial autonomy. Steinbeck's *Of Mice and Men* explores this struggle for financial autonomy among ranch-hands. However, while the ranch-hands often seem powerless over their circumstances, individuals such as Curley's wife and Crooks offer an insight into marginalised demographics who, in 1930s America, were more powerless still.'

Theme/Paragraph One: Among the men on the ranch, there is a dichotomy between the management – Curley and his father – who have the luxury of economic autonomy, and the ranch-hands, who are disempowered by their meagre means.

- The Salinas Lettuce Strike of 1934 – a strike that saw unionists in Salinas, California strike for higher wages, only to have their efforts mercilessly quashed by the local sheriff – was profoundly illustrative of the state of affairs at the time: the management held all the cards, whereas efforts by farm labourers to assert themselves were rapidly snuffed out. Steinbeck was deeply aware of this particular strike (it inspired his *In Dubious Battle*, 1936), and the power differential between management and labour can be seen in *Of Mice and Men*, too. [*AO4 for invoking historical and literary context that is relevant to the discussion at hand*].
- Shortly after Lennie and George arrive at the ranch, they encounter 'the boss': a 'fat-legged man' who 'wore high-heeled boots and spurs to prove he was not a labouring man'. Not only does his aloof moniker ('the boss') telegraph his power, but so too does the symbolism of his writing Lennie and George's names

in his ledger ('the names were entered in the book'): in the same way a writer ultimately has power over his characters' fate, the 'boss' has control over his ranch-hands' economic fate. [*AO1 for elaborating on my theme and invoking relevant quotations to buttress my argument*].

- Central to Lennie and George's dream of purchasing a 'little house and a couple of acres' is a modicum of economic autonomy – the ability to stop working at their own discretion to, say, visit 'a carnival or a circus...or a ball game'. Interestingly, Steinbeck, by giving George and Lennie the opportunity to include Candy, place the protagonists within touching distance of this independence: Candy, with his lifetime of earnings and compensation for a dismembered hand, has the funds to make this ambition feasible. Steinbeck seems to be acknowledging that such autonomy is *not* impossible for men in their position; though, crucially, the chances of securing it are vanishingly small. [*Further AO1 for adding complexity to the argument and, again, deploying textual evidence*].

Theme/Paragraph Two: Crooks and Curley's wife, however, have even less control over their circumstances. Curley's wife's diatribe aimed at Crooks suggests that she only has control over those below her in the pecking order.

- Lorna Moon in Clifford Odets's *Golden Boy* (1936) – another bleak text about Depression-era America – is portrayed as systematically disempowered: she escapes poverty only due to her fiancé's benevolence; she is constantly excluded from his place of work; and her attempt to strike out on her own at the play's end leads to her death. [*AO4 for invoking literary context that is relevant to the discussion at hand*].

- If Odets's text is an attempt to chart the ways women were rendered powerless by the patriarchal power structures of the time, so too is Steinbeck's. For while the male itinerant workers are disempowered by their economic circumstances, more powerless still is Curley's wife, a character's whose very name points to her lack of autonomy. When venting to Lennie in Chapter Five, the degree to which her survival has depended on men becomes painfully clear: she talks of a man who 'was in pitchers' who had 'promised to put [her] in the movies' – yet while this is the fate she had coveted, she had had no capacity to pursue this ambition herself. Moreover, in the wake of her failure to enter film, the only power left to her had been, ironically, the power to choose which man instead she would depend on for survival: 'So I married Curley'. [*AO1 for elaborating on my theme and invoking relevant quotations to buttress my argument; AO4 for enhancing my argument with relevant historical and artistic context*].
- Interestingly, Curley's wife is presented as being in a position of power at only one point – namely, during her abuse of Crooks. Indeed, she explicitly boasts of the power of life and death she wields over him – 'I could get you strung up on a tree' – and her repeated use of the word 'n*****' invokes the heritage of slavery, where black people were literally owned by whites. This interaction reveals that, in this world in

which women have limited power, black people seem to have even less: Crooks is subjugated to someone whose very name connotes subjugation, his very room colonised by white bodies, his very selfhood 'reduced...to nothing'.[1] [*Further AO1 for adding complexity to the argument and, again, deploying textual evidence; AO4 for enhancing my argument with relevant historical context*].

- In 1930s America, although slavery had been abolished, there remained deep segregation (known as the Jim Crow laws) that systematically disempowered black people in practically all areas of life – from schools, to housing, to public transport. As a result, it is perhaps unsurprising that Steinbeck should present Crooks as the character in *Of Mice and Men* most at the mercy of his circumstances. [*AO4 for enhancing my argument with relevant historical context*].

Theme/Paragraph Three: Although Lennie has access to means of meagre economic advancement, he is powerless to control the circumstances of his mental state. George, on the other hand, is rendered powerless by his moral obligations to Lennie.

- In a 1937 article in *The New York Times*, Steinbeck revealed that he based Lennie on a real person who was 'in an insane asylum in California right now', and whom Steinbeck had witnessed killing a foreman because 'the boss had fired his pal'. Interestingly, however, whereas this real-life individual's violence seems to have been motivated by anger, Steinbeck strives to portray Lennie's violence as accidental. In the immediate aftermath of Lennie's bust-up with Curley (which leaves Curley with a mangled hand), Lennie balefully protests that he 'didn't mean no harm'. This phrase encapsulates the predicament of Lennie's existence: though his intentions tend to be benign – he doesn't 'mean' any 'harm' – he is, as a result of his severe intellectual disability, powerless to regulate his own actions or manage his own lack of inhibitions. [*AO4 for invoking historical context that is relevant to the discussion at hand; AO1 for elaborating on my theme and invoking relevant quotations to buttress my argument*].

- As a result, Lennie's colossal physical power takes on deeply ironic connotations: for all his strength, he is a powerless, child-like figure. After killing Curley's wife, Lennie is momentarily oblivious to what he has done: 'I don't want to hurt ya' he says with childlike sincerity. Lennie, we conclude, is powerless to regulate his own reactions; powerless to control the circumstances of his own mental state. [*Further AO1 for adding complexity to the argument and, again, deploying textual evidence*].
- George often posits how he would be thriving without Lennie: 'If I was alone I could live so easy' is his near constant refrain. Yet while this may be true, George is governed by a profound moral obligation to Lennie; and as long as this circumstance of obligation persists, George remains powerless over his own fate. Lennie, then, is a presence that impinges both on his own freedom, but also George's. [*Further AO1 for adding complexity to the argument and, again, deploying textual evidence*].

Conclusion

Roosevelt's New Deal led to the establishment of a litany of organisations and the passage of many, many bills. You do not need to know them all. That said, having some specific knowledge up your sleeve about them can be really useful. Here, I'm using just such knowledge as the centrepiece of my conclusion.

> 'In 1935, Roosevelt passed the National Labor Relations Act; but while a key step in granting workers autonomy – it laid out how businesses ought to interact with labour and set out unions' bargaining rights – farmworkers were excluded from its provisions. Even as Roosevelt was granting workers piecemeal empowerment, then, the farmworkers of the ilk populating Steinbeck's novels were left behind. Perhaps it is unsurprising, then, that Slim – an individual portrayed as having unique sway among the workers – paradoxically seems to draw his power from his philosophical understanding of their collective powerlessness in face of utilitarian realities, as exemplified by his verdict that Candy's infirm dog ought to be killed for its own good.'

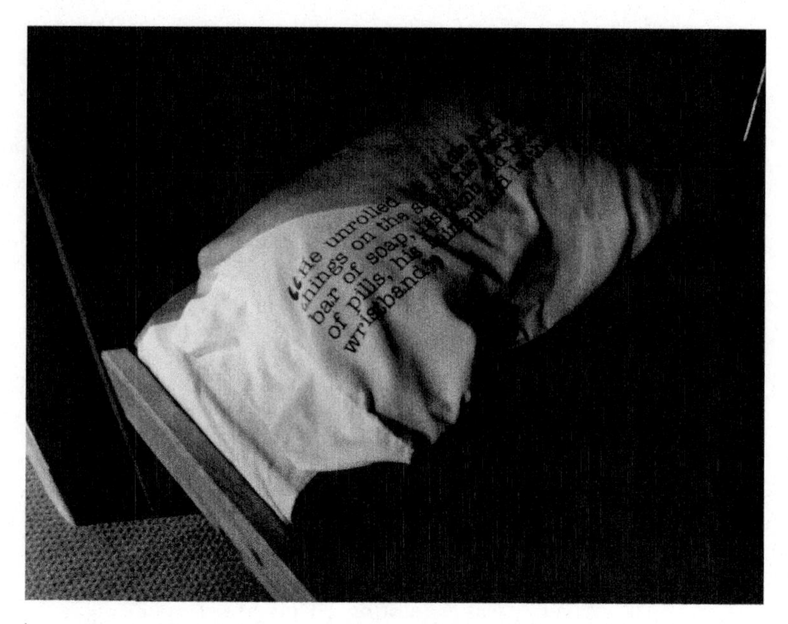

A bunk-bed in the The National Steinbeck Center, Salinas, with a pillow bearing a quote from *Of Mice and Men*.

ESSAY PLAN FIVE

HOW IS THE CHARACTER OF CANDY IMPORTANT IN OF MICE AND MEN?

INTRODUCTION

By now, you can see there is a pattern to writing introductions. First, I hit the AO4 criteria. Next, I pivot to thematic discussions. It's a one-two punch: AO4 then AO1. Yes, we are jumping through hoops; but frankly, to succeed at GCSE, you need to accept that a bit of hoop-jumping is required.

'Though Franklin Roosevelt had been battling polio since 1921, throughout his presidency (1933-1945) he strove to conceal the extent of his illness: he ensured he was never publicly seen in a wheelchair, for instance, and relentlessly played down the severity of his paralysis. If the America Roosevelt inhabited was one that equated disability with weakness, it is perhaps unsurprising that Steinbeck casts Candy – the one-handed old swamper in *Of Mice and Men* – as an ostracised figure who bears the brunt of ageist and ablest sentiments.[1] Yet Candy is significant in more subtle ways: he adds depth to Lennie and George's tragedy and functions as a mouthpiece for misogyny.'[2]

Theme/Paragraph One: Candy serves a crucial narrative function in the novel: as a result of his savings, he allows George and Lennie to get within touching distance of owning property, thereby deepening the sense of tragedy once their plans go awry.

- In Chapter Three, after hearing George and Lennie daydreaming about their plans to secure a property, Candy offers to contribute his savings (some 'three hunderd an' fifty bucks'), thereby placing George and Lennie just a month's earnings away from realising their ambitions: 'I bet we could swing her for that' George asserts and even goes so far as to 'write to them old people' from whom he is planning to purchase it. With Candy on board, then, Lennie and George's seemingly far-fetched ambition is suddenly transmuted into something far more tangible and immediate.[3] [*AO1 for elaborating on my theme and invoking relevant quotations to buttress my argument*].
- The animating message at the heart of Steinbeck's novel is that the so-called American dream – the idea that, through hard work, one might achieve economic autonomy – is a cruel chimera in Depression-era America. By using Candy to allow these three men (against all odds) to get within touching distance of success, then snatching away the prize, Steinbeck acts to deepen the tragedy around their failure. Moreover,

Candy's personal disappointment magnifies the overall sense of tragedy. In the wake of Curley's wife's death, we are told that for Candy to acknowledge that their dream is dead is tantamount to speaking 'his greatest fear'. [*AO4 for invoking historical context that is relevant to the discussion at hand; further AO1 for adding complexity to the argument and, again, deploying textual evidence*].

- While Roosevelt passed legislation that sought to provide aid for the elderly (The Social Security Act, 1935), it excluded farm workers, and thus an individual such as Candy would have fallen through the cracks. Candy's exclusion from a financially secure retirement reflects the real-life plight of elderly farm-labourers of the time, and is used by Steinbeck to underscore his central message: that no matter how long or hard individuals struggled, financial autonomy almost always remained beyond reach. [*AO4 for invoking historical context that is relevant to the discussion at hand; further AO1 for adding complexity to the argument*].

Theme/Paragraph Two: Steinbeck uses Candy to explore society's ablest and ageist biases.

- Some of the most scathing language used in the novel is levelled not at a human, but at Candy's dog: Carlson claims that he knows 'nothing that stinks as bad' as Candy's dog; that he 'can't stand him'; and that, because of the dog's 'rheumatism' and lack of 'teeth', 'he ain't no good to [Candy]' nor 'himself'. [*AO1 for elaborating on my theme and invoking relevant quotations to buttress my argument*].

- However, while the dog – *not* Candy – is the immediate target of these comments, Candy is of course symbolically intertwined with his dog, and Carlson's comments reflect wider sentiments towards the aged and disabled that apply to the human world, too. Interestingly, shortly after Carlson executes Candy's dog, Candy brings up his dog to George and Lennie – 'You seen what they done to my dog' – before, a couple of sentences later, reflecting how he 'wish't somebody' would 'shoot' him once he becomes too old to work. The proximity of these comments subtly conveys that Candy understands how the ageism and ableism used to justify putting down his dog apply also to him. Certainly, ableism in particular was especially rampant in California, where eugenics laws were on the books from 1908; and as sterilisations ramped up in the first three decades of the twentieth century, California saw the most forced sterilisations of disabled people of any single US state (some 20,000). [*Further AO1 for adding complexity to the argument and, again, deploying textual evidence; AO4 for enhancing my argument with relevant historical context*].
- Whereas the ableist and ageist sentiments of the ranch-hands are arguably more subtle, Curley's wife is far more explicit. In Chapter Four, she derogatorily refers to Candy as 'a lousy ol' sheep' and asserts that, if he dared to call her out for lying, his word would be considered lacking in credibility: 'Nobody'd listen to you'.[4] [*Further AO1 for adding complexity to the argument and, again, deploying textual evidence*].

Theme/Paragraph Three: While Candy may be on the receiving end of Curley's wife's abuse, Candy for his part also levels vitriol at Curley's wife, and thus gains significance as a mouthpiece for societal misogyny. Steinbeck uses their dynamic to illustrate how society pits ostracised peoples against each other.

- 1930s America was a realm where female sexuality was constantly policed: in Hollywood, for instance, after films such as *Design For Living* and *Queen Christina* (both 1933) strove to candidly explore female sexuality, the reactionary The National Institute of Decency from 1934 onwards began purging films of any content that presented women in a sexually suggestive manner – quite literally policing the portrayal of women in art. [*AO4 for invoking historical and artistic context that is relevant to the discussion at hand*].
- Certainly, the way Candy seeks to condemn and police Curley's wife's sexuality is deeply reminiscent of these contemporary reactionaries. Before we encounter Curley's wife, our understanding of her is powerfully mediated through Candy's scathing assessment of her to George and Lennie: not only does he call her a 'tart' – a word that seeks to shame Curley's wife for her sexuality – but he also explicitly instructs his interlocutors to view her through this derogatory lens: 'look her over mister. You see if she ain't a tart.'[5] His words echo the sentiments of those contemporary Hollywood censors who were manipulating how viewers perceived women.[6] [*AO1*

for elaborating on my theme and invoking relevant quotations to buttress my argument; AO4 for invoking historical and artistic context that is relevant to the discussion at hand].

- Certainly it is true that Curley's wife is not without significant flaws: her racial abuse of Crooks is profoundly alienating, and she is cruel to Candy and Lennie, too. However, in the wake of her death, it is striking that Candy does not grant her even a modicum of sympathy. Instead, he cruelly persists in deriding her for her sexuality: he labels her a 'God damn tramp' and, again, a 'tart.' Indeed, that he lays the blame for the derailing of his ambitions solely at Curley's wife's feet (' Ever'body knowed you'd mess things up') implicitly suggests she is deserving of this fate and smacks of extreme misogyny. [*Further AO1 for adding complexity to the argument and, again, deploying textual evidence*].

Conclusion

Sometimes AO4 marks can be gained not by referring to a particular event or work of art, but by meditating convincingly on the nature of the era under discussion. This is the approach I've taken in this conclusion.

> 'That Candy is, by occupation, a ranch hand, yet is missing a hand, is deeply ironic: the disability might be considered a metaphor for the violence wrought by economic structures on individuals such as Candy. Yet if Candy is important as a way of exploring the chimera of the American dream and the unique plight of the

elderly and the disabled in 1930s America, he is also significant insofar as he reveals societal misogyny. It is particularly interesting, however, that Curley's wife – another ostracised individual – is not only the one whom Candy singles out for abuse, but is also the one who most virulently articulates ableist and ageist sentiments. This reveals how the harsh, dog-eat-dog world of 1930s America pitted ostracised people against one another.'

The only image on record of Franklin Roosevelt in a wheelchair. Copyright © FDR Presidential Library & Museum.

ESSAY PLAN SIX

HOW DOES JOHN STEINBECK PRESENT THE RELATIONSHIP BETWEEN LENNIE AND GEORGE IN OF MICE AND MEN?

Introduction

The Wall Street Crash is pivotal to understanding Steinbeck's work, so do make sure you have a working knowledge about it!

'In 1928, the year prior to the Wall Street Crash, the then President-elect Herbert Hoover coined the phrase 'rugged individualism' – an expression intimately linked to a philosophy of radical independence from government that was drawn from the American frontier, and which underpinned Hoover's *laissez-faire* economic policies.[1] By choosing to place a tight-knit duo of itinerant workers at the centre of *Of Mice and Men* – a team, a partnership – Steinbeck's novel arguably functions to rebuff the mantra of rugged individualism.[2] Yet his presentation of Lennie and George's relationship – particularly George's sense of duty to Lennie – also provokes questions regarding moral obligations and the way these obligations can impinge on personal freedoms.'

Theme/Paragraph One: Steinbeck presents Lennie and George's relationship as a counterpoint to the philosophy of rugged individualism.

- At one point in Chapter Two, Slim, after learning about Lennie and George's long-term friendship, muses how there 'ain't many guys travel around together'. Later, he reiterates his incredulity at this set-up: he notes that its 'funny' how the pair of them 'string along together' and how he has 'hardly never seen two guys travel together', noting instead how most men in their position 'go out alone' and 'never seem to give a damn about nobody'.[3] In Slim's formulation, rugged individualism is the norm, whereas a duo like Lennie and George's is anomalous. Moreover, Steinbeck, by having Slim note how these solitary men never 'give a damn' about anyone else, seems to insinuate that rugged individualism is, at its core, a selfish doctrine, which suggests in turn that there is an underlying virtue to Lennie and George's mutual loyalty. [*AO1 for elaborating on my theme and invoking relevant quotations to buttress my argument; AO4 for invoking historical and cultural context that is relevant to the discussion at hand*].
- Indeed, George and Lennie self-consciously define themselves in opposition to this selfish, individualistic mindset, conceiving themselves instead as a team: 'I got you to look after me, and you got me to look after you', Lennie observes in Chapter One. [*Further AO1*

for adding complexity to the argument and, again, deploying textual evidence].

- It is striking, however, that despite their friendship offering a more virtuous counterpoint to rugged individualism, the two men's plans still go awry. Steinbeck's message is a deeply fatalistic one: namely, that while a duo may offer an emotional and spiritual succour that a one-man-band lacks, it is still unable to guarantee financial success in the harsh economic wilderness of Depression-era America. [*AO4 for invoking historical and cultural context that is relevant to the discussion at hand*].

Theme/Paragraph Two: Steinbeck presents the preservation of the relationship between George and Lennie as a moral obligation for George, but also something that limits him.

- Although George does seem to have genuine affection for Lennie, Steinbeck ultimately presents their relationship as predicated on George's sense of moral obligation. While confiding in Slim, for instance, George notes how he and Lennie are entangled via their mutual history – 'him and me was both born in Auburn. I knowed his Aunt Clara' – and details how profoundly ill-equipped Lennie is to fend for himself: George tells a historical anecdote about how Lennie almost drowned after George told him to jump in a river, and a second (more recent) anecdote in which, after panickedly clutching onto a woman's 'red dress', Lennie wound up being run out of town – as George puts it, Lennie 'gets in trouble alla time'. Implicit is these comments is George's sense of moral duty to his companion: he must stick around to protect Lennie from himself. [*AO1 for elaborating on my theme and invoking relevant quotations to buttress my argument*].

- Certainly, George's sense of moral duty to help his fellow man could be seen as an endorsement of the philosophy of Herbert Hoover's chief political adversary, and the victor of the 1932 Presidential Election, Franklin Roosevelt. Roosevelt's economic policies, unlike Hoover's, emphasised the moral need of government to intervene to help those struggling economically ('We are going to make a country where no one is left out', he famously asserted), and his radical New Deal initiated unprecedented government spending to achieve this aim. [*AO4 for enhancing my argument with relevant historical and artistic context*].
- Yet while Roosevelt's spending might be construed as moral, it also required self-sacrifice by the nation: between 1933 and 1936 public debt as a percentage of GDP approximately doubled. Similarly, though George's friendship with Lennie built on obligation does serve to benefit George in certain specific ways (Lennie, after all, offers George the balm of companionship), Steinbeck nevertheless presents it as something that limits George and involves self-sacrifice. Time and again, George expresses how much easier his life would be without Lennie: 'I could get along so easy...if I didn't have you'. [*AO4 for enhancing my argument with relevant historical and artistic context; further AO1 for adding complexity to the argument and, again, deploying textual evidence*].

Theme/Paragraph Three: When it comes to the mechanics of how George and Lennie's relationship is presented, although the novel is rendered in the third person, Steinbeck has George take responsibility for curating and presenting his and Lennie's relationship to the world.

- While Franklin Roosevelt's polio was publicly known, he strove to hide the extent of his paralysis from the public eye: he ensured he was never seen publicly in a wheelchair, and he taught himself to walk small distances in leg braces. Roosevelt, in short, understood the importance of public appearance, and thus, by his own design, there developed a gulf between his lived reality and how he was perceived. [*AO4 for invoking historical context that is relevant to the discussion at hand*].
- Although Steinbeck's novel is relayed in the third person (and thus the third person narrator has no small impact on how Lennie and George are presented to the reader), when it comes to how their friendship is presented to the rest of the *dramatis personae*, George takes a Rooseveltesque lead in curating its appearance, understanding the importance of managing how his friendship with the disabled Lennie is perceived. Shortly after George and Lennie arrive at the ranch, the boss quizzes the pair, and George tells the boss (falsely) that Lennie is his cousin: 'He's my.... cousin. I told his old lady I'd take care of him'. The fact they are not in fact cousins is less important here than the fact George is asserting his power to curate how their friendship is presented.

That beforehand George repeatedly instructed Lennie to remain silent during this interaction is telling: George, not Lennie, takes the lead in this act of curation. [*AO1 for elaborating on my theme and invoking relevant quotations to buttress my argument*].

- When conversing with Slim in Chapter Two, George again strives to curate his and Lennie's friendship, framing it as a force for good: 'It's a lot nicer to go around with a guy you know'. George, then, not only curates their friendship's appearance, but strives to present it (and indeed Lennie himself) as something benign and non-threatening. [*Further AO1 for adding complexity to the argument and, again, deploying textual evidence*].

Conclusion

I know that GCSE students have loads on their plates and the point of a guide like this, up to a point, is to feed you information regarding historical context, so you don't need to go rummaging for it yourself! That said, the films of Charlie Chaplin are genuinely quite fun, so if you get a chance, do consider watching a couple!

'At one point in Charlie Chaplin's iconic 1935 film, *Modern Times*, his Tramp is sucked into the gears of a machine: a metaphor for the ways in which the capitalist system's philosophy of rugged individualism mercilessly churns up the solitary worker. However, while Lennie and George's friendship in *Of Mice and Men* is presented as a counterpoint to the brutality of this kind of solitary struggle – an oasis of companionship – Steinbeck tellingly still ensures his pair are defeated by the system that mauls Chaplin's Tramp: their friendship offers succour, but not salvation. Yet just as important as the way their relationship is presented is *how* it is presented, with Steinbeck casting George as a curator who strives to manage how the duo are perceived.'

A mural in Vevey, Switzerland. It is a recreation of the iconic scene in Chaplin's *Modern Times* in which Chaplin's tramp is swallowed into a factory's machine.

ESSAY PLAN SEVEN

HOW IS THE CHARACTER OF SLIM IMPORTANT IN OF MICE AND MEN?

Introduction

'Looming large in the American imagination is the idea of the noble frontiersman: an individual with the skill to weather the harsh frontier, and the virtue to righteously expand the American project:'full of action, full of manly pride and friendship', as Walt Whitman put it in his 1865 poem 'Pioneers! O Pioneers!'. Slim in *Of Mice and Men* might be construed as a version of the idealised frontiersman transplanted into an ultra-brutal version of the frontier that has been scoured of any of its romantic sheen. Yet if Slim is significant as a symbol of the idealised frontiersman, he is significant also as George's confidante, Steinbeck using Slim to grant readers an insight into George's mind.'

Theme/Paragraph One: Steinbeck uses Slim as a sounding board for George: Slim allows us to understand George better and gain an insight into his history. Slim, then, is used by Steinbeck as an expositional mechanism.

- Throughout the Great Depression, President Roosevelt made innovative use of radio technology to conduct what were dubbed 'fireside chats' – these were more informal addresses to the nation that sought to bring calm in the midst of ongoing economic tumult. While the technology of course only allowed one-way communication, the public consciousness of these addresses invited Americans to consider the importance of intimate conversations: of sharing problems and dialoguing. [*AO4 for invoking historical context that is relevant to the discussion at hand*].
- In many respects, Slim is important because he allows George to engage in what might be described as a proverbial 'fireside chat'. Near the start of Chapter Three, the reader sees Slim subtly coax George into opening up and sharing more about his history: we are told, for instance, that Slim's seemingly innocent conversation starter – 'funny how you an' him string along together' – is in fact imbued with a tone that seeks to draw George out: 'It was Slim's calm invitation to confidence'. Sure enough, George begins to open up, thereby granting the reader crucial insights into (among other things) his historical relationship with Lennie ('Him and me was both born in Auburn') and the recent goings-on in Weed (where they sent 'a party out to lynch Lennie'). Slim, then, is

pivotal in drawing George out, thereby furnishing the reader with crucial exposition. [*AO1 for elaborating on my theme and invoking relevant quotations to buttress my argument*].

- That George's guarded and cautious nature is reiterated time and again in the novel's opening pages – he fiercely reprimands Candy, for instance, when he fears Candy might be eavesdropping on his conversation with Lennie in Chapter Two – adds greater emphasis to Slim's importance as someone capable of loosening George's lips. [*Further AO1 for adding complexity to the argument*].

Theme/Paragraph Two: Slim is a fatalistic philosopher. He is not responsible for the way the world is – indeed, on a personal level, he has kindness and sympathy for his fellow man – but he understands the cruelty of the world too well to try and fight it.

- As Candy's dog's life hangs in the balance in Chapter Three, it is striking that the men *en masse* – and without any explicit consultation – defer to Slim's opinion and treat his verdict as decisive ('Slim's opinions were law'). More interesting still, however, is Slim's verdict itself: he decides that the infirm dog 'ain't no good to himself' and ought to be put down, and caps his verdict with the aside that he would pick the same fate for himself: 'I wish't somebody'd shoot me if I got old an' a cripple'. [*AO1 for elaborating on my theme and invoking relevant quotations to buttress my argument*].

- In the opening scene of Clifford Odets's *Golden Boy* – another 1937 text that grapples with the hardships of Depression-era America – Lorna Moon voices a fatalism that befits the time: 'it's the Twentieth Century, Tom – no more miracles'. Slim – like Lorna – is not devoid of sympathy: he empathises with Lennie and kindly gives him a dog, and, after Lennie's death, he helps George 'to his feet' both literally and metaphorically. His verdict on Candy's dog, rather, is borne not of malice, but of a profound fatalism: Slim understands that in the cruel, utilitarian, dog-eat-dog world in which they exist, it is futile to try and fight its ways, and there is wisdom in capitulation (just as Lorna in Odets's play sees wisdom in marrying the man she does not love, as opposed to fighting to be with the man she does). Slim's final words to George at the novel's close reiterate his belief in their collective powerlessness over their circumstances: he tells George he had no choice but to kill Lennie: 'You hadda'. [*AO4 for invoking literary and cultural context that is relevant to the discussion at hand; further AO1 for adding complexity to the argument and, again, deploying textual evidence*].
- There is irony, then, in the way Slim's opinions are treated as 'law', for while this implies a power over the other men, in reality Slim's verdicts are predicated on the acknowledgement of their collective powerlessness. [*Further AO1 for adding complexity to the argument and, again, deploying textual evidence*].

Theme/Paragraph Three: Slim is in some respects an ideal frontiersman: the paradigm of the skilled individual.[1] That he is beneath the likes

of Curley is used by Steinbeck to illustrate how perverse this society is.

- The legendary nineteenth century gunslinger, Wild Bill Hickok, occupied a unique place in the American imagination as the epitome of the noble frontiersman. His ethical code aside, he was also renowned for his physical prowess; and while it was true that he did have genuine talents as a shooter, the release of three fawning biographies in the 1930s served to wildly exaggerate this legacy in the public imagination. [*AO4 for invoking historical and cultural context that is relevant to the discussion at hand*].
- As a physical specimen, Slim might be said to embody a frontiersman in the mould of the Hickok of the popular imagination. From the moment he appears, the narrator places reverent focus on Slim's physical prowess: we are told, for instance, that 'he moved with a majesty only achieved by royalty and master craftsmen'. Moreover, there is enormous focus on his precision ('he was capable of killing a fly on the wheeler's butt with a bull whip'), which again aligns him with the lionised marksmen of the frontier. That these words of reverence emanate from the narrator, and not an individual character, hint that the sentiments may in fact be Steinbeck's own. Slim, then, is important insofar as he represents an ideal of frontier physicality that was synonymous for many (including, arguably, Steinbeck) with nobility. [*AO1 for elaborating on my theme and invoking relevant quotations to buttress my argument*].
- Yet while Slim may embody the frontiersman ideal, he does not inhabit the frontier in its ideal form; rather,

Steinbeck's is a perverted, topsy-turvy version of the frontier in which this craftsman, who by all rights ought to be the 'prince of the ranch', is lower in the pecking order than the sadistic upstart Curley.[2] This bastardisation of the rightful order is arguably Steinbeck's way of pointing out how the frontier of the 1930s could no longer deliver on the promise of vast opportunity that so defined it in popular lore. [*AO4 for enhancing my argument with relevant historical and cultural context*].

Conclusion

'Even prior to the Great Depression, the frontier was understood to be as much a brutal space as it was one teeming with opportunities: in Charlie Chaplin's 1925 film, *The Gold Rush*, his pioneering Tramp finds himself so down on his luck that he is forced to eat his own shoe. Yet Steinbeck uses Slim to expose a harsher version of the frontier: one in which attempting to prosper at all is futile, and in which skills which were once considered sacrosanct – craftsmanship, physical prowess – are no longer able to deliver economic autonomy. Nevertheless, Steinbeck uses his reverent description of Slim's physical prowess to telegraph the intrinsic virtue of the skillset of the jerkline skinner.'

Chaplin's Tramp eating a shoe in the 1925 film *The Gold Rush*.

ESSAY PLAN EIGHT

HOW ARE ANIMALS PRESENTED AS IMPORTANT IN OF MICE AND MEN?

Introduction

'Mark Twain's 1903 short story, 'A Dog's Tale', by endowing a canine with the power of narrative creation and charting the inhumanity of man, marked a unique attempt in American literature to explore the parallels and proximity between man and beast. While Steinbeck's *Of Mice and Men* does not make use of a first-person animal narrator, not only does the Robert Burns poem from which it draws its title nod to symmetries between man and beast, but the novel is also populated by animals (both literal and metaphorical) that invite us to make such comparisons. Animals are integral to decoding Lennie; further, the ruthlessness of the animal world functions as a metaphor for the ruthlessness of the ranch.'

Theme/Paragraph One: Animals, both literal and imaginary, are used by Steinbeck as a means of granting insight into Lennie's innermost nature.

- Although Lennie is cast as an individual uniquely incapable of expressing himself, Steinbeck offers alternative mechanisms to grant the reader insight into Lennie's nature. In the opening chapter, after George chastises Lennie for keeping 'a dead mouse', Lennie expresses his motive for carrying it: 'I could pet it with my thumb while we walked'.[1] Yet while encoded in this desire to 'pet' this animal is a warmth and abundance of love, it clashes with the outcome of these sentiments: Lennie's affection winds up killing the mouse: 'you've broke it pettin' it'. This pattern, we learn, has repeated itself many times in the past: Lennie's Aunt Clara 'stopped givin' 'em to' him because Lennie 'always killed 'em', George notes. Indeed, this pattern repeats itself later in the novel: Lennie ends up killing Slim's puppy while 'playin' with him'. [*AO1 for elaborating on my theme and invoking relevant quotations to buttress my argument*].
- If the author uses literal animals, then, as a tool to convey a key facet of Lennie's nature (namely, that he is full of love, yet a love that is dangerously out of control), Steinbeck also uses imaginary animals – that is, the rabbits on the hypothetical future property – as a means of exploring Lennie's ambitions and longings. In Maurice Kains 1935 guide to homesteading, *Five Acres and Independence* (a self-described practical guide), particular focus is paid to rearing rabbits on the farm: rabbits, in other words, were seen as symbolic shorthand for the aspiration to own property, which

had become ingrained in the American psyche as a sacrosanct right in the wake of the 1862 Homestead Act. Steinbeck uses the symbol of rabbits, then, to allow the simple-minded Lennie to articulate his homestead longings: 'Tell me...about the rabbits'. [*AO4 for enhancing my argument with relevant historical, literary and cultural context*].

Theme/Paragraph Two: Steinbeck depicts the animal kingdom as a Darwinistic battle-ground. The parallel between the animal kingdom and human life on the ranch – the former becomes a metaphor for the latter – invites the reader to consider man's own animalism.

- In the opening moments of the final chapter, the reader is exposed to a shocking Darwinistic dance unfolding in the natural world: we are told that a 'water snake glided smoothly up the pool' to the 'legs of a motionless heron', before a 'silent head and beak lanced down' and 'swallowed the little snake'. Interestingly, however, when Lennie arrives at the brush moments later, he is described as moving 'as silently as a creeping bear'. This simile, as well as the timing of Lennie's arrival, is Steinbeck's means of intimating that he intends this Darwinistic vignette to be taken as a reflection of human existence. [*AO1 for elaborating on my theme and invoking relevant quotations to buttress my argument*].
- It is significant to note that in the 1890s, the Yale academic William Sumner was delivering lectures outlining his beliefs in Social Darwinism: a theory

predicated on the idea that Darwin's notions of "survival of the fittest" apply to humankind as well. In the ensuing decades this belief became increasingly mainstream: it is touted, for instance, by the brutish Tom Buchanan in F. Scott Fitzgerald's *The Great Gatsby* (1925). [*AO4 for enhancing my argument with relevant historical, literary and cultural context*].

- Steinbeck's message appears to be a bleak and sombre acknowledgement that human interactions had become just this kind of struggle. His ranch is a ruthless, Darwinistic battle-ground. There is a near-constant sense of impending violence and power struggle: Curley from the off is spoiling for a fight ('Curley's just spoilin''); Whit salivates at the thought of a showdown between Curley and Slim ('I'd like to see this'); and Curley attacks Lennie shortly after – to name but a few examples. Moreover, just as the simile likening Lennie to the bear cemented a sense of parallelism between man and beast, the other individuals on the ranch are also constantly likened to animals: Candy has 'whiskers' and is a 'lousy ol' sheep'; Curley is 'like a terrier'; Curley's wife is 'like a fish' – the list goes on. The animal kingdom, then, is of utmost importance in the novel: its Darwinism and ruthlessness functions as a metaphor for human existence. [*Further AO1 for adding complexity to the argument and, again, deploying textual evidence*].

Theme/Paragraph Three: Candy's dog is significant as a foreshadowing device, but also as a way to explore ageist and ableist sentiments within the ranch.

- Candy's dog takes on outsized significance in the novel due to the foreshadowing role it plays in Lennie's death: both are executed via a gunshot to the head. Unlike Lennie's death, Candy's dog's death takes place off-stage: we are told simply 'a shot sounded in a distance'. This narrative choice ensures the sequence increases the sense of tension, without eclipsing the drama of the on-stage execution of Lennie in the final chapter. [*AO1 for elaborating on my theme and invoking relevant quotations to buttress my argument*].
- However, while Candy's dog plays an important prefiguring role, its significance is more multifaceted still. Because of the parallels in their fates, one is invited to see Candy's dog as symbolically linked to Lennie, while also linked (via its old age and disability) to Candy himself. As a result, the way Candy's dog is treated might be seen as capturing sublimated feelings towards Candy and Lennie as avatars for the physically infirm and the mentally disabled respectively.[2] As Candy's dog's life hangs in the balance in Chapter Three, then, and Slim opines that the 'dog ain't no good to himself' and adds that he 'wish't' somebody would shoot him if he 'got old an' a cripple', one could read into these comments a prevailing attitude not just towards animals, but towards disabled and elderly people in general. [*Further AO1 for adding complexity to the argument and, again, deploying textual evidence*].
- Certainly, this utilitarian attitude tallies with the sentiment at the time: support for eugenics was gathering steam in the States in the early twentieth century – so much so that 1923 saw the inception of

The American Eugenics Society, and by the mid 1930s there had been some 20,000 forced sterilisations. Disabled people of the time, then, were construed as lesser-than-human, as though akin to animals. [*AO4 for enhancing my argument with relevant historical context*].

Conclusion

Another valid way of scoring AO4 marks is to discuss aspects of the author's life that might help us better understand the book. This is the approach I have taken in this conclusion.

> 'The opening paragraphs of *Of Mice and Men*, which deal exclusively with a natural tableau populated by 'rabbits', ''coons', 'deer' and a 'lizard' is (unlike the rest of the novel) written in the present tense: Steinbeck seems to be signalling with his structural and narrative choices here that we should keep alert to the natural world and the critters therein. Given Steinbeck's own personal reverence for the animal world – 'In some areas Charley is more intelligent than I am', he once asserted about his pet poodle – it is perhaps unsurprising that Steinbeck casts animals – both literal and metaphorical – as central to decoding and deciphering his novel.'

John Steinbeck with his dog Charley. Copyright © Luiyo

PART TWO: WJEC STUDENTS ONLY

EXTRACT BASED QUESTIONS

Out of respect for the fact that *Of Mice and Men* remains in copyright, we shall not be reproducing extracts in their entirety. Instead, we shall indicate how the extracts start and finish so students can track down the passages in question.

EXTRACT QUESTION ONE

This extract is taken from Chapter One. It starts with: **'"George – why ain't we goin' on to the ranch and get some supper?"'** It finishes with: **'"You get another mouse that's fresh and I'll let you keep it a little while."'**

In the Penguin 2017 paperback edition of the novel, this extract appears on pages 9 to 11. However, your edition may differ.

Look closely at the way George speaks and behaves here. What does it reveal about his character? Refer closely to the extract in your answer.

As George grapples with Lennie's fixation with the corpse of a dead mouse in this extract, he reveals many facets of his personality: his core of kindness and empathy; his tendency to succumb to frustration; and his self-possession.

Your introduction should quickly indicate that you understand what is happening in the passage, then outline the topics you intend to discuss. We are, essentially, using a thematic approach once more!

Shortly after Lennie departs at the start of the extract, and George realises he is trying to surreptitiously retrieve his mouse, George soliloquises empathy for his companion's hopeless fixation and lack of guile: '"Poor bastard," he said softly.' Whereas the word 'bastard' – a kindly colloquialism – hints at George's empathetic mindfulness of Lennie's status as a spurned and ostracised individual, the word 'softly' seems to both describe George's volume but also his tone: he is a man with the capacity to feel softly. Indeed, even the sternness George exhibits on Lennie's return – 'You know God damn well what. I want that mouse' he snaps in response to Lennie's equivocations – arguably connotes kindness: he understands that the mouse is unclean (he 'washe[s] his hands' after touching it) and seems to ardently believe that he must be cruel to be kind: 'I ain't takin' it away jus' for meanness'.[1]

In extract-based answers, we need to ensure we are engaging in close language analysis, so we can secure AO2 marks. Notice how I hone in on the meanings and nuances of individual words. This is essential.

Nevertheless, though George displays kindness, he also exhibits a proclivity to frustration. This is best embodied in the insults he levels at Lennie near the passage's end. The phrase 'You crazy fool' is self-contained in a short, sharp sentence that distils the frustration, and is followed by exclamation-pointed insults and incredulity: 'Blubberin' like a baby! Jesus Christ!'

To hit the very top grades for AO2, you need to also be aware of form and structure, so notice how I comment on sentence length as a means of hitting this criteria! Notice also how I am alert to punctuation.

That George 'wheeled about' before his second tranche of insults emphasizes the suddenness of his frustration – his mood, like his body, has done a proverbial three-sixty – as well as its ferocity: it seems to be momentarily spinning (or wheeling) out of control. Yet it is telling that his frustration is so quickly displaced again by kindness, as shown by the warm 'hand on Lennie's shoulder': while prone to frustration, George's kindness and empathy ultimately win out.

Notice how I am constantly taking short, sharp quotes from the passage. This is absolutely key: after all, it telegraphs to the examiner that you are focusing intently on the passage's nuances.

At the start of the passage, George spells out his reason for waiting a night before arriving at the ranch: 'I'm gonna lay right here and look up. I like it'. With this comment, George reveals not only a decisiveness, but also a degree of self-possession that borders on recalcitrance: he knows he is expected at the ranch, but he is engaging in a small act of defiance by giving himself a night's respite.[2] It could be argued that this decision points to a selfish streak – after all, Lennie is yearning for 'supper at the ranch' – though this respite benefits Lennie, too. George's decisiveness is also telegraphed through his willingness to issue instructions ('you get wood') and his body language: his hand is described as 'outstretched imperiously'.

A modern-day landscape in Soledad, California — near where Steinbeck's novel is set. Copyright © Jim Bahn

EXTRACT QUESTION TWO

THIS EXTRACT IS TAKEN FROM CHAPTER THREE. IT STARTS with: **'The door opened. Slim came in, followed by Curley and Carlson and Whit.'** It finishes with: **'Then Curley attacked his stomach and cut off his wind.'**

In the Penguin 2017 paperback edition of the novel, this extract appears on pages 62 to 63. However, your edition may differ.

Look closely at the way Curley speaks and behaves here. What does it reveal about his character? Refer closely to the extract in your answer.

This sequence, which sees Curley on the defensive with Slim before instigating a physical confrontation with Lennie, showcases Curley's cowardice and insecurity, while also granting insight into his profoundly volatile disposition.

You can score AO2 marks not just by looking closely at individual words, but also at phrases, as I've done in this paragraph with my commentary of Curley's use of double negatives.

About midway through the passage, Carlson observes how Curley 'tried to throw a scare into Slim', but in fact 'Slim throwed a scare inta [Curley]'. This analysis invites the reader to see Curley's behaviour at the start of the passage – namely, his attempts to appease Slim – as an exercise in cowardice. Twice Curley insists he 'didn't mean nothing' by asking Slim as to the whereabouts of his wife, the repetition emphasizing the eagerness to appease, and the double negative ('didn't' clashes with 'nothing') making it seem as though he is scrambling out his words. Moreover, that he 'hung close to [Slim's] elbow' physically implies an eagerness to please: he is stumbling after Slim to apologize and mollify. However, if Curley's frantic attempts to appease Slim suggest cowardice, perhaps even more so does his fighting style later in the extract. Even though Lennie is frozen in fear and not fighting back – 'Lennie's hands remained at his sides', we are told, and he 'bleated with terror' – Curley only continues his assault ('Curley attacked his stomach and cut off his wind'). As Curley doubles-down on his unprovoked assault on the terrified, child-like Lennie, Steinbeck emphasizes his cowardice.

That Curley initiates a physical altercation in the first place suggests a profound volatility in his nature; however, this is signalled in other ways throughout the passage. For example, Curley's attention rapidly flits from one potential opponent to another: Curley, we are told, 'whirled on Carlson' (the word 'whirled' hinting at both a rapid physical motion, but also kaleidoscoping emotions); next, he 'glared' at Candy; then (in the very next sentence) 'his eyes slipped on past [Candy] and lighted on Lennie', the quick succession of sentences emphasizing the rapidity of Curley's shifts in focus. Moreover, shortly after, the narrator likens Curley to a 'terrier' – the animal simile emphasizing Curley's lack of emotional control – and notes that 'Curley's rage exploded', with 'exploded' emphasizing the shocking escalation in Curley's emotional state. As Curley's attention flits wildly, then, and he exhibits disorientating mood-swings, we are left with an impression of radical volatility.

You will notice here that, after observing the words used, I also make a point about sentence structuring, so that I'm hitting the exam board's structure/form criteria.

Lurking beneath Curley's outburst in this passage, it might be noted, is a powerful sense of insecurity. As he sets upon Lennie, Curley insists that 'No big son-of-a-bitch is gonna laugh at me' and that he will 'show ya who's yella'. The phrase 'big son-of-a-bitch' bluntly gestures to Curley's inferiority complex stemming from his short stature, which manifests in the form of antagonism towards larger men, whom he resents. His repetition of the word 'yella' here – a word that Carlson levelled at him earlier in the passage – gestures to a second of his insecurities: that

It's great when analysing language to point out specific language techniques used – such as the use of a simile I've picked up on here. However, if you bring in a technique, you *must* also comment on its effect, otherwise you will not score the marks!

however cowardly he might be, Curley cannot abide to be thought of as such (though, ironically, his attempt to dispel the notion by attacking Lennie in fact only cements it further).

An image of "Wild" Bill Hickok, whose violent exploits in the nineteenth century became synonymous with frontier life.

EXTRACT QUESTION THREE

This extract is taken from Chapter Four. It starts with: **‘"I guess somebody's out there," Crooks said.’** It finishes with: **‘"I seen too many guys with land in their head. They never get none under their hand."’**

In the Penguin 2017 paperback edition of the novel, this extract appears on pages 74 to 75. However, your edition may differ.

How does John Steinbeck present the character of Crooks here? Refer closely to the extract in your answer.

As Lennie and Candy assemble in Crooks's room, Steinbeck uses this sequence as an opportunity to explore Crooks's character: the ways in which he has been brutalised by his circumstances, his profound cynicism, and his yearning for social contact.

Throughout this extract, there is evidence that Crooks has been brutalised – that is, been made brutal – by his status as the ranch's lone black man. This is telegraphed through the adverbs describing his speech – 'shortly', 'irritably,' 'brutally' – but also through his words. In response to Candy's compliment about his room, Crooks replies not warmly, but with a sardonic riposte: 'And a manure pile under the window. Sure, it's swell.' The 'manure pile' might be seen as symbolic of the circumstances that have brutalized Crooks: he has been forced to put up with no small amount of metaphorical 'manure'. Further, the way Steinbeck condenses Crooks's sarcastic 'Sure, it's swell' into a short, sharp sentence lends it an extra layer of steeliness and edge.

Be alert to symbolism: it can really help bolster your argument. Also, notice at the end of this paragraph how I make a quick point about sentence length. Scoring those structure/form marks need not be complicated!

The way Crooks mercilessly pours cold water on Candy and Lennie's ambitions near the extract's end not only again points to the way he has been brutalized (he is not interested in sparing feelings), but also points to a profound cynicism. Crooks opines that 'You'll talk about it a hell of a lot, but you won't get no land'. Not only does his use of the double negative ('won't' clashes with 'no') add

Notice how I'm pursing a thematic approach. Each paragraph covers a new theme/topic, allowing me to pair my language analysis to broader concerns.

emphasis to the sentiment, but his use of the word 'hell' (which he repeats again later in the paragraph) also subtly conjures a sense of doom that enhances his cynicism. Crooks assertion that Candy will be a swamper till he is taken out in a 'box' – a particularly blunt synonym for a coffin – also captures Crooks's cynicism: he feels certain Candy's future will be bleak and undignified; that he will be eternally boxed-in by his circumstances. Yet while Crooks's cynical tone is difficult to escape, it might be argued that he would be more accurately described *not* as a cynic, but as a realist: someone who has 'seen too many guys' and understands the harsh realities.

Notice how, when I bring in a quote, I indicate to the examiner where in the passage I'm taking it from. Not only does this orientate the examiner, but it also makes me look as though I am in control of the material.

For all Crooks's guardedness, however, Steinbeck also hints that Crooks harbours a yearning for social interaction and companionship. His aside about Slim near the passage's start – 'Slim's a real skinner. He looks out for his team' – speaks volumes: implicit here is that, in Crooks's eyes, what makes Slim authentic is his loyal companionship to his fellow man ('he looks out for his team'). Later, he notes how Slim has made time for him personally ('Nobody been here but Slim'). The subtext to all this is that Crooks respects Slim precisely because Slim acknowledges the yearning for companionship in his fellow man (Crooks included). When Candy enters Crooks's room, we learn that 'It was difficult for Crooks to conceal his pleasure with anger'. While Crooks's 'anger' points to a guardedness, his 'pleasure' points to a secret yearning for just this kind of social interaction. Likewise, there is a sorrow in his observation that 'Guys don't come into a colored man's room very much': the way he refers to himself in the third person ('a colored man') telegraphs his profound sense of isolation and separation.

An image of the exterior of a movie house in Mississippi, USA, in 1939. A staircase points up to an entrance for black attendees, whereas the door under the stairs is labelled 'White Men Only'.

EXTRACT QUESTION FOUR

This extract is taken from Chapter Five. It starts with: **'The sun streaks were high on the wall by now, and the light was growing soft in the barn.'** It finishes with: **'In a moment Candy came back, and George was with him.'**

In the Penguin 2017 paperback edition of the novel, this extract appears on pages 91 to 92. However, your edition may differ.

How does John Steinbeck create mood and atmosphere here? Refer closely to the extract in your answer.

In this sequence, which comes just after Lennie departs the stables in which he has killed Curley's wife, Steinbeck artfully works to create a tragic and disquieting atmosphere; though, at the passage's close, the atmosphere becomes one of impending trouble.

> This question focuses on mood and atmosphere rather than a specific character, which can be tricky. I've broken it down into three themes: namely, the three different, competing moods Steinbeck has created. Then, in each paragraph, I've drilled into specifically how Steinbeck has created each of these moods.

Steinbeck uses a number of tactics to create a tragic atmosphere in the barn. Near the start of the passage, we learn that 'the light was growing soft in the barn': the dimmed lights create a mournful, contemplative air, while the verb 'growing' almost seems to personify the light, as though it is consciously choosing to pay respects. Working in tandem with this mournful dimming is the muffling of ambient sound: not only is it 'very quiet in the barn', but it seems to become more quiet still: the 'voices of the men in the game seemed to grow more quiet'. In recognition of the tragic import, the sound is muted, creating an atmosphere akin to a mournful moment of silence. Moreover, Steinbeck artfully elongates the unfolding of time: we hear that a 'moment settled' and 'remained for much more than a moment'. Paradoxically, in this formulation, a moment becomes more than a moment – time, in acknowledgement of the tragedy, is temporarily on pause. However, if Steinbeck uses light, sound and time to create a tragic atmosphere, he also does so by honing in on the lost potential of Curley's wife: 'she was very pretty and simple, and her face was sweet and young.' Steinbeck uses two couplets of adjectives ('pretty and simple'; 'sweet and young') to place emphasis her underlying innocence, youth and aesthetics, inviting to reader to contemplate what has been lost.

Alliteration is always a good technique to point out. However, as mentioned already, if you are commenting on a specific technique, you must ensure you are also commenting on its effect.

However, while Steinbeck works to create a tragic mood, he also strives to create a disquieting atmosphere, too. This is perhaps best achieved via the 'shepherd bitch' and her reaction to Curley's wife's body: her 'hair', we are told, 'arose along her spine' – the alliteration on the letter 'a' creating a verbal ripple mimicking the rippling hair – and 'whimpered and cringed'. This base, primal reaction, in which the dog is plainly deeply unsettled, is offered up as a prompt to the reader, conjuring an atmosphere of disquiet. Moreover, Steinbeck uses Candy to further enhance the atmosphere of disquiet. Steinbeck, by having Candy first reprimand Curley's wife ('You oughten to sleep out here'), makes use of dramatic irony: the reader, of course, already knows Curley's wife is not sleeping.[1] Yet this moment of misunderstanding serves to delay and thus amplify Candy's disquiet when he finally realises the truth: 'then he was beside her and- "Oh, Jesus Christ!"' That the narrator is cut-off mid-sentence (as signified by the dash) by Candy's blasphemous utterance emphasizes Candy's shock, and further enhances the atmosphere of disquiet.

Although for the most part Steinbeck creates a sombre atmosphere in this passage, at the very end he strives to create a mood of brewing trouble. The horses are perhaps his most effective way of producing this mood: they 'stamped and snorted' – the sort of body language that suggests violence and confrontation, and this is emphasized through alliteration – and they 'clashed their chains of their halters'. Aside from being a menacing sound in itself, the word 'clashed' is again evocative of violence and confrontation.

A small ranch in eastern California — evocative of the sort of buildings we encounter in *Of Mice and Men*. Copyright © Don Graham

NOTES

ESSAY PLAN ONE

1. An itinerant worker is a worker who travels from place to place for employment.
2. To vicariously experience something is to experience it indirectly through someone else.
3. A third person narrative is when you have a narrator telling the story – as in Steinbeck's novel – and it sounds a bit like this: 'he went there'; 'she did this'. A first person narrative, on the other hand, is when the story is told from the point of view of one of the characters. 'I went there'; 'I did this'.
4. A soliloquy is when a character is alone and expresses their feelings out loud.
5. To eschew something is to reject it.
6. A dogma is a set of ideas or principles.
7. Sacrosanct means something akin to holy.
8. To transgress means to violate or 'go beyond'.
9. Jim Crow refers to a set of laws that existed up until 1965 and which systematically encoded discrimination against black people into American institutions.
10. A microcosm is a small version of something larger.

    A patriarchy is a society run by and controlled by men.
11. Willy Loman is the main character in Arthur Miller's 1949 play, *The Death of a Salesman*. This play is another exploration of the hollowness of the American Dream.

ESSAY PLAN TWO

1. Denouement is another word for climax.
2. Antebellum America refers to America prior to the American Civil War (which took place between 1861 and 1865).
3. A chimera is something we might hope exists, but is in fact illusory.

ESSAY PLAN THREE

1. In Margaret Atwood's The Handmaid's Tale (1985), set in a dystopian America, all the handmaids are named after the men to whom they belong. The protagonist is called Offred – that is, Of Fred – since she 'belongs' to a man called Fred.
2. To be an avatar of some idea of concept is to be a symbol of that idea or concept!
3. Animus is another word for hostility.
   To pillory someone is to attack or mock them.
4. A diatribe is an angry, ranting speech.
5. To dehumanise someone is to deny or minimise their humanity.

ESSAY PLAN FOUR

1. To be subjugated by someone is to be conquered by that individual, or brought under their power.

ESSAY PLAN FIVE

1. Ageism is a bias against elderly people, whereas ableism is a bias against disabled people (be they physically disabled or mentally disabled).
2. Misogyny refers to a hatred of women.
3. Transmuted means something similar to transformed.
4. Derogatory language is language that is degrading or offensive.
5. An interlocutor refers to someone being addressed. In a way, *you* are my interlocutor as you read this sentence!
6. A censor is someone who removes and silences content from artistic works. The word can also be used as a verb: to censor someone is to silence them.

ESSAY PLAN SIX

1. Laissez-faire is a French term and it means 'to leave alone.' It is often used by economists to describe how the capitalist system works: the government is encouraged to simply leave things alone, and let the free market determine how things pan out.
2. A mantra is another word for a slogan.
3. To be incredulous is to almost be disbelieving and surprised.

ESSAY PLAN SEVEN

1. A paradigm is another word for model.
2. To be sadistic is to take pleasure in other people's pain.

ESSAY PLAN EIGHT

1. To chastise means to tell off.
2. Sublimated feelings are sort of like secret feelings: feelings that are being revealed indirectly.

EXTRACT QUESTION ONE

1. To equivocate is to talk in an indirect, roundabout way.
2. To be recalcitrant means to be rebellious.

EXTRACT QUESTION FOUR

1. Dramatic irony is when the reader knows something that a character does not.

Printed in Great Britain
by Amazon

83824751R00061